The Songs of a wolf

– 45 songs in search of a singer –

Martin J. White

Hafan Books

Published in Swansea by Hafan Books (hafanbooks.org) in 2021

ISBN 9781916044272

Available at www.lulu.com/hafan

Contact Martin at martinjohnwhite@googlemail.com

Hafan Books is a non-profit publisher associated with SASS (Swansea Asylum Seekers Support). SASS is a community group run by refugees, asylum seekers and other local people. All profits from Hafan Books go to SASS. For information about Hafan Books and SASS, visit sass.wales and hafanbooks.org or email t.cheesman@swansea.ac.uk

Printed by Lulu.com

Layout and cover design by Martin White and Tom Cheesman

Thanks to:

     Damon Peters; Tom Cheesman and all my friends at SASS;
     Phil Broadhurst and all the staff at Oxfam Castle Street, Swansea.

Contents

Introduction

My singing voice is not to be inflicted on the world; had I the temerity even to warble these songs in the shower, the tiles would form an escape committee, tear the shower curtain into strips to make a rope and climb out of the window, risking the shattering drop to the pavement below...

Nonetheless, these are indeed Songs (with 'bridges' in *italics*) not just lyrics - a few even exist as primitive recordings: a voice (not mine!) acoustic guitar & tape hiss, in roughly equal proportions. They deserve their chance to go out into the world: there is even a Hit waiting to be uncovered; work out a tune for 'Fall Into The Sun' (uncannily, the first piece in this book) give it some Oasis drive & bite and surely it's a smash!

As a songwriter, my idols are Bob Dylan, Neil Young, Leonard Cohen, Joni Mitchell and the like: who *can* compose the short and sweet - but tend towards longer and (by accident and/or design) much more poetic excursions. Of course, I make no claim to belong in such exalted company, but hope that the book at least may help a worthwhile cause.

I like the idea of earning money with my songs as anyone would who has lived in poverty & dressed in rags; and if it should occur to a musician or a music publisher that there is good material herein to be taken on, great: it would be immensely satisfying to get some recognition for decades of steady creative work. Even so (and believe it or not!) my nirvana would not be the receipt of a large dollop of cash, but to turn on a radio one day and hear one (or more!) of my songs floating over the ether ...bring it on.

My previous book recorded the fall-out of a relationship that crashed and burned - those who read it were assured my next would be less bleak, but there's still perhaps a mournful undercurrent in places. Strange - it's not as if the state of the planet or humanity gives any cause for concern, is it?

I make no apology for a recurring theme of longing to escape - preferably to sunnier climes. This is surely forgivable on the part of someone living and working in Swansea (the graveyard of umbrellas) who has slogged through the murk & drear of no less than 28 winters in what is now the officially accredited rainfall capital of Britain...

(N.B. - To make full use of space, a few lyrics have been compressed using the / sign to indicate the presence - or absence! - of line breaks.)

Alphabetically,
this book
is dedicated to:

Albert, Alyson, Bunny, Christian, Hugo, Jenni, Kate, Maya & Percy

If loving is the tender trap
We'll take that chance and not turn back

Fall Into The Sun

You don't belong in winter
Sleeping underneath the snow
You don't belong in darkness
'cause the bright lights call you so
You don't belong where hearts are cold
And love can never grow
You know you'd sooner fall into the sun…

It's time to be a gypsy
When the southlands call to you
It's time to be a gambler
When you've nothing left to lose
It's time you lived a diff'rent life
And one that gets you through
Or else you'd better fall into the sun…

And I wish I could go with you on your journey
I wish we had the wings so we could fly
On into the sun until we melt away
Better that than try to live a lie…

You've got to be a changeling
Or a silkie from the sea
You've got to be an orphan
Though you do relate to me
You've got to be so far from here
And find what sets you free
You know you're bound to fall into the sun…

You don't belong in winter
Sleeping underneath the snow
You don't belong in darkness
'cause the bright lights call you so
You don't belong where hearts are cold
And love can never grow
You know you'd sooner fall into the sun….

Wolf Song

When I was first a wolf
And hid my heart away
I'd curl a lip and bare my fangs
To keep the world at bay
And I didn't even know that I was running
But at least
As a wolf
I could run…

When I became a wolf
Because of childhood hurt
I spurned most signs of friendliness
And kept my language curt
And I couldn't help but know that I was aching
But it seemed
That to ache
Was my fate…

But I fell to a girl
Who didn't turn and run
Who came up close and touched my face
And warmed me like the sun
And I hadn't even known that I'd been crying
But at least
In those years
I could cry…

So I withdrew my claws
To spare her gentle face
In awe at what her heart could do
And of her poise and grace
And I hadn't realised that I was loving
Because love
Was something
I'd not known…

Then I became a man
And gave your world its chance
To pull me in and draw my fangs
And whirl me in its dance
And I couldn't see the danger of such dreaming
'cause at least
For a while
I could dream…

So I became a fool
And tried to play the game
Of taking more than my fair share
While others got the blame
And I didn't even know that I was sleeping
'cause at least
Till guilt came
I could sleep…

Then I looked at the world
And how it is these days
And wondered why I'd tried so hard
To 'humanize' my ways
'cause I couldn't help but see that I was falling
Into depths
So empty
But so cruel…

So I'm a wolf again
Refuse to play a role
That mode of life styled 'civilized'
had tried to steal my soul
But I understood in time that I'd been faking
And a wolf
Never needs
To be fake….

High Time

When the road goes through the flatlands
You're dreaming of the mountains
Dreaming of that one place
Where the air is crystal clear
And feeling that it's high time
Your life revealed its purpose
With all the questions answered
And nothing left to fear…

When you're on the desert highway
You're longing for the ocean
Longing for a rhythm
That can rock away your doubt
And saying that it's high time
You faced up to the rat race
You've got your head together
And know what life's about…

High time
You saw things clearly
High time
For telling true
High time
To let the world see
The best there is in you…

Though you're destined for the city
Your heart is in a small town
Heart is with a circle
Who won't let you crash and burn
And knowing that it's high time
You went and took the prizes
The sooner that you get there
The sooner you'll return….

That Flame Inside

Free minds / Will learn to speak softer
Evade the hunter's snare
So easy / To be marked as a suspect
By revealing you still care
That from evil being done
There's almost nowhere left to run…

Wild things / Will have to run faster
If they want to survive
Real feeling / And the instinct for freedom
Seeming barely alive
In the eyes of those who know
There's almost nowhere left to go…

Though we run to breathe and hide to be
It's enough, so long as you're with me
And if loving seems a tender trap
We'll take that chance and not turn back

We'll take that chance and not turn back
And rescue something from the wrack…

Our lives / An act of sedition
Against the Stepford quo
Their offer / Of a future as zombies
One we should overthrow
And we'll keep that flame inside
Till we no longer have to hide…

New love / A kind of defiance
Where hope has worn so thin
Two people / Quite surrounded by madness
Somehow able to grin
Though they both can clearly see
There's almost nowhere left to be…

Run, breathe, hide to be / what other future can you see?
Run, breathe, hide to be / what other future can you see?
Run, breathe, hide….

Living For The Moment

Too often when you think of love
You're trying to hold on
To something real and vivid
You can see and yet it's gone
I loved you 'cause you turned to me
And kissed me in the rain
I'm living for the moment
You take that chance again…

Too often when you think of love
It's fading out of sight
An old romantic movie
A world that's black and white
I loved you for your crazy laugh
The way you made things fun
I'm living for the moment
You break through like the sun…

The start is always easy
You could treat love as a game
And say when I was serious
You didn't feel the same
But I knew when you loved me too
My heart felt what had stirred
And we were fooling no-one
Though we never used the word…

Too often when you think of love
You're caught up in the past
Recalling something fragile
That could never hope to last
I loved you when you came to me
As naked as a flame
I'm living for the moment
You start that fire again….

Into The Blue

Now the sun is rising
In the sky and in your mind
The clouds are miles below you
And you feel you've broken through
Things that overwhelmed you
Simply fading like bad dreams
…because you're flying
And you're gone into the blue…

Too long spent in shadows
In your life and in your heart
With someone else's failure
Always weighing down on you
Now that's all behind you
And you're thinking for yourself
…that's why you're flying
And you're gone into the blue…

Into the blue
That tastes of freedom
Into the blue
that's like a friend
Into the blue
That holds the future
Into the blue
That never ends…

Dreams you thought would never
Come to life and come to be
Will get the chance to play out
'cause they mean so much to you
Nothing is beyond you
Now you're doing what feels right
…because you're flying
And you're gone into the blue…

…because you're flying
And you're gone into the blue….

Cadillac Moon

(for Jean-Michel Basquiat)

Cadillac moon
Cadillac moon
High and unnoticed since late afternoon
Telling nothing a mysterious rune
Bright in the sky as the hope in the womb
A soft-glowing fabric fresh from the loom…

Cadillac moon
Cadillac moon
The silver streaming across the lagoon
Your night of glamour your Hollywood tune
The swish of silk as she enters the room
Her smart remark in the caption balloon…

Cadillac moon
Cadillac moon
Trouble's coming and it's coming real soon
Picks out the one who thinks he's immune
City of angels and engines that croon
Those golden streets where the nuggets are strewn
Someone else's bust is always a boom
Sci-fi distances the spice in the dune
The greed for water the desert in bloom…

Cadillac moon
Cadillac moon
Sinking low now as the flame and the spoon
Bright in the sky as it's dark in the tomb…

Cadillac moon
Cadillac moon
How much life hurts though it's like a cartoon
Her goodbye words in the caption balloon
Trouble's coming and it's coming real soon
Heading back east and the airplanes go vroom
Feeling the itch in the never healed wound
Painting those skulls unaware of your doom
Her goodbye words, oh the flame and the spoon
Cadillac moon
Cadillac moon….

Distances

You could be riding a thermal
Or half-drowned in a flood
You could be catching a wave into Bondi
Or somewhere stuck in the mud…

You could be walking on sunshine
Or wond'ring what went wrong
You could be sharing your life with a film star
Or waking next to King Kong…

All these distances
You could travel
And never leave my heart
You could be having
The time of your life
Oh my love, I hope you are…

I hope you are…

You could be climbing a mountain
Or halfway to your dreams
You could be crowing 'bout how things have worked out
Or regretting hopeless schemes…

You could be taking it easy
Or struggling to unwind
You could be living the dream in some penthouse
Or ground floor losing your mind…

You could be making a fortune
Or wearing all you own
You could be counting your winnings in Vegas
Or wond'ring how you'll get home…

You could be over the ocean
Or up there with the stars
You could be dining with premiers and princes
Or somewhere stuck behind bars….

Mirror Blues

What happened to that skinny kid
Who always had a smile
And always used to be around
But now it's been a while
Who used to be good company
And he had a certain style…

What happened to the open face
That launched so many schemes
And always had such energy
To back his crazy dreams
Who used to be so positive
But he's gone or so it seems…

Each morning in the mirror
I'd see him looking back
Shrugging off the loneliness
And all the things he lacked
I don't know if I buried him
Or just drove him away
But you know that I'd give ev'rything
To be like him today…

What happened to that future world
Where people would be free
And always live the way they chose
It hasn't come to be
And if you look in the mirror
Who's the person that you'll see….

August Night At The Monkey Café

August night at the monkey café
Drum and bass
And the room starts to sway
Pretty people
Just doin' what's cool
They got it down
Like a new golden rule…

Feeling light behind baby blue eyes
Born to win
And your star's on the rise
Giving glances
Till you see the one
Who's cold as ice
And as hot as the sun…

Drum and bass
It's the sound of the city
Drum and bass
It's the feeling in the street
Drum and bass
It's the rhythm of all rhythms
The rhythm of the rhythm
Of the place where rhythms meet…

Sun is up and you never went home
Alley cat
With an instinct to roam
Finding freedom
For now anyway
That's how it is
At the monkey café….

Rising Star

You flew out to Los Angeles
And spoke to all the suits
They all admired your music
And said that you were cute
Someone's working out a contract
They'll never let you roam
But it's hard to live on promises
Eight thousand miles from home…

You went into the studio
And filmed some promo clips
They all seemed so supportive
And yet the time just slips
Someone's setting wheel's in motion
You've only got to wait
But it's hard to stomach empty words
Two days since you last ate…

But they won't get you down / 'cause you know who you are
When all the clouds have rolled away / You'll be a rising star…

You wonder what else you can do
How else to make them see
You only need that green light
To set your talent free
Someone's checking trends and fashions
And what brings in the cash
But if they would simply back you up
You're bound to be a smash…

You flew out to Los Angeles
And sang to your guitar
They all admired your music
And swore you would go far
the suits all say you're bound to win
Your voice is heaven-sent
But it's hard to bank on flattery
When you can't pay the rent….

Alone With Love

An orphan by choice
And hated by some
Not asking too much
But bound to pay for things not done…

Fall into the trap
That caring creates
If you're making bonds
You tempt all kind of vengeful fates…

Wanted the love / that I'd seen in the movies
When it came / I didn't understand it
If it's true / such moments are forever
You must know
A love like ours could never die
Love like ours could never die…

Sought only to live
And cause no-one pain
Not wanting to be
The one left standing in the rain…

'cause one day unplanned
You come into style
I'm hoping it's true
You've found at last that loving smile….

Now I need time / to contemplate my failure
For so long / to be a human being
And I don't ask / for anyone's forgiveness
All I want
Is just to be alone with love
Just to be alone with love…

I lucked into silk
And didn't know why
I wasn't left out
But lifted to the highest high….

Futures

Dream yourself through walls
Into hidden spaces
Dream yourself through flaws / And find a gift to give
Make yourself the thought
That brings a smile to faces
But don't forget to love
'cause then you'll want to live….

Slide between the bars
Get outside the system
Slide between the blades / That want to cut you down
Make yourself the thought
That fills a world with longing
But don't forget to breathe
Though so afraid you'll drown…

When the future sees the proof
How some refused to face the truth
They're gonna think us pretty strange
And those who don't abet the crime
Still have to do the time
All in hope that something's gonna change…

Stand outside of time
See a diff'rent image
Stand outside of rules / They've set to break your heart
Make yourself the thought
That brings a sense of freedom
And when the world needs hope
It's then you'll play your part…

Flout the laws of men
Made to mask the guilty
Flout the plans of those / Who want to make us pawns
Make yourself the thought
That stirs the urge for justice
But don't forget to share
That's how the new day dawns….

Shapeshifter

Shapeshifter
You were hiding out in plain view
The way some kinds of beauty
Almost always go unseen
Calm and elfin on that rise
The future in another's eyes
Heaven in a world that's got so mean…

Shapeshifter
Finding each time you'll be diff'rent
The magic working outwards
As you open up your heart
And when other hopes are bust
So glad it's me you've learned to trust
Never dreamt I'd get the hero's part…

Shapeshifting / How we strive to elude
The grasping hands / Of the brutal and crude
Learn to be vague / While telling no lies
Resist the claims / That we rightly despise…

shapeshifter
Sunburst day I fin'lly found you
The feast of lupercalia
We were breathing our own cloud
There was something I could hear
Above your warning words so clear
Never knew my heart could beat so loud…

Shapeshifter
You are my lover and my twin
The substance and the meaning
Something radiant and true
Till our time has ceased from flowing
And our minds have stopped from knowing
Never doubt the love I have for you….

American Gods

The Jesus of the Rio Grande
Took a bullet through each hand
Killed by vigilante cops
While he helped the meek
While he helped the meek
But still he'd walked on water
Reached down to a drowning man…

The Jesus of the Rio Grande
Left for dead upon the sand
Rose again, the morning sun
For those who believed
For those who believed
Ready to walk on water
Reach down to a drowning man…

American gods are stern and forbidding
American gods like to lay down the law
American gods don't do forgiveness
You can see who invented
These gods and what for…

The Jesus of the Rio Grande
Entering the promised land
Blamed in politicians lies
Hiding their own faults
Hiding their own faults
Though they'd seen him walk on water
Try to save a drowning man…

The children of the lesser gods
Want to cross the river
Told they'd find the promised land
On the other side…

Who made the promise?
Who did they make the promise to?

Who made the promise?
Who did they make the promise to?

Down At The Corner (The Right Stuff)

Down at the corner
The kids still meet and dream
Dream of something better
Somewhere new and clean…

Under the neon
The headlights flare and show
Sometimes one gets lucky
Knows which way to go…

Where grown-up lies can't hurt
Or stain you with their dirt
And you can make this world seem new
By making love that's true…

Out in the darkness
The future sometimes sparks
If you have the right stuff
To swim amongst the sharks…

If you've got the moves
To get into that groove
If you've got the smarts
To touch a million hearts…

Down at the corner
The kids still meet and dream
Dream of something better
Somewhere never seen…

Where grown-up lies can't hurt
Or stain you with their dirt
And you can make this world seem new
By making love that's true….

Ghost In The Shell

Ghost in the shell
Neither real nor dream
Haunted by the human
Never knowing what to feel…

Wakes in the mind
Neither steel nor blood
Floating in an ocean
Relives fantasies of birth…

What can you hold
That they can't scatter?
And if you can't keep
A few mem'ries clear
A sense of yourself
Will it matter?

Ghost in the shell
Cyborg that can hope
Guardian of a future
Where our hearts are still as dark…

Slave to a role
Someone else imposed
Held back as you're reaching
For a destiny you seek…

Ghost in the shell
Melting out of sight
Haunted by the human
Rarely certain what's for real…

Haunted by the human
Never knowing what to feel…

Ghost in the shell
Ghost in the shell
Guardian of hope
Never knowing what to feel….

Howling At The Moon

The moment always has to come
One day the cupboard's bare
The strongest can be brought to tears
By something that's not there
Crying like a baby / Like a child that's dropped his spoon
When his secret stash is used up
He'll be howling at the moon…

The biggest bullies bite the dust
One day they have to fall
Be all washed up and toothless now
With no-one scared at all
Moaning like a bus queue / Tuneless songs that drunkards croon
When the whisky's out their system
They'll be howling at the moon…

The moment that should never come
One day she couldn't stay
Although it tore you both apart
It had to be that way
Whining like a junkie / Because love can end too soon
When you can't hide it from yourself
You'll be howling at the moon…

The greatest gambler gets it wrong
Someday he'll lose his shirt
The empire built up in his dreams
Gone headlong in the dirt
Has to speak more softly / Like a fool who's changed his tune
And since I chose the losing hand
I'll be howling at the moon…

The moment always has to come
One day the cupboard's bare
And then we simply have to laugh
To show we just don't care
Goofing like an actor / Who's been asked to play the loon
And purely for the hell of it
We'll be howling at the moon….

Black Mirror

In a black mirror
You face no contradiction
Your asked to show no papers
And no statement can be proved
You're opening to feeling / And ready to be moved…

Find a new rhythm
A slight change of direction
You'll leave the past in storage
get the urge to travel light
Streaming through the darkness / Another form of flight…

Black mirror / Where you never see yourself
And even less / The one you'd like to be
Wide river / No discriminator
Each life reflected / As it's carried to the sea…

In a black mirror
Your image might be perfect
Your dreams might have a future
And you'll never see the flaws
Never see a doubtful look / Hear nothing but applause…

Black mirror / Where you never see yourself
And even less / The one you'd like to find
Wide river / No discriminator
Each life reflected / As it's slipping out of time…

In a black mirror
Your avatar is driving
You're moving through a city
Where each vivid thought comes real
And wearing someone's halo / Not fazed by what you feel…

Black mirror / Moonless, tideless ocean
Black mirror / Deep and endless sea
Black mirror / Moonless, tideless ocean
Black mirror / Somewhere else to be…

Black mirror / Black mirror….

Starsailor

It's a blue afternoon
And I'm thinking about you
how you searched for the dolphins
And sailed amongst stars
your voice a seduction
Used to healing and stealing
Away from this old world
To rise and fall so far…

The song of a siren
And you're sinking in quicksand
but your voice has no limits
Finds its own way through
Your songs incantations
Full of aching and breaking
Away from this old world
To be somewhere that's new…

Starsailor / Born to be restless
You took all the risks going / Had to see what's true
Starsailor / Known to be reckless
Pushed too hard too often / You left this world too soon…

It's a song slowly sung
And another strange feeling
And it comes on so lonely
A blue melody
Your words full of warnings
Against faking and taking
An easy road over
The one that sets you free…

It's a blue afternoon
And I'm thinking about you
How you searched for the dolphins
And sailed amongst stars
Your voice like the honey
Used for healing but stealing
Away from this old world
To travel on so far….

Work And Dreams

We didn't know we'd gambled
But it seems we lost our shirt
And the politicians promise us
Ev'ry kind of hurt
The poorest are to lose the most
But all must take a hit
Well, all except the guilty ones
Who dropped us in the pit…

Now it's ten years down the line
And the cuts don't lose their bite
We might accept the medicine, but
Something isn't right
If we're all in this together
Why don't they wield the axe
On thieves right at the very top
Who still evade their tax?

One law for the rich
Another for the poor
They say it's always been like that
And justice can be bought
By those who have the money
To tip the scales their way
And the rich are cutting Legal Aid
So justice
Justice is a game…

Many people's work and dreams
Swept away like so much dust
But the nature of this system is
Always boom and bust
So if we don't move to change it
For one that can sustain
Then just as people start to hope
It will crash and burn again….

Sunday Morning Early

Sunday morning early / When the world has ended
Wake up and smell the coffee / It's time to make a choice
Yesterday is roadkill / Beside an endless highway
It isn't time for list'ning / It's time to use your voice…

Something breaks the silence / Seems it wasn't fatal
The asteroid passed over / The dinosaurs still walk
From a diff'rent aeon / You're on another wavelength
There isn't a translation / It isn't time to talk…

Nothing's so seductive / As routine and habit
Before you've got your boots on / They've dealt another hand
Going in a circle / Of work and drunken laughter
But don't take consolations / It's time to make a stand…

Go out to the desert / Get away from people
Can say that you feel lonely / But it isn't really true
Where your heart feels easy / It soars just like an eagle
Space and heat-haze shimmering / Are things that get you through…

Pick out the clothes for trav'ling
It may not be too late
Still time to take a risk or two
Still time to set the date
Still time to kiss the only one
Time to celebrate…

Sunday morning early / Life is no rehearsal
Wake up and smell the coffee / It's time to face the day
There can be a future / But only if you seize it
It isn't time for waiting / It's time to walk away…

One day soon you'll notice / Your sky hasn't fallen
The stars are where they should be / Hank Williams is still king
You'll pick up your guitar / And play the chords that haunt you
It could be a beginning / It could be time to sing….

Hoping To Forget

I came down the highway
With nowhere to belong
To start again with little
But street-corners and a song…

So I took to playing / On sunny days for change
Hoping to forget my own heart / While I tell you 'love is strange'…

We all take wrong turnings
And sometimes there's a cost
And turn our backs on real love
No idea what we've lost…

So we take to playing / Life's self-deluding games
Hoping to forget a darkness / Where there used to be a flame…

Didn't have the answers
And so I couldn't stay
Disappointment in her eyes
And the guilt drove me away…

So we take to running / From things life puts us through
Hoping to forget our own hurts / While we're singing 'love is blue'…

I came down the highway
With nowhere to belong
To start again with little
But street-corners and a song…

So I took to playing / On sunny days for change
Hoping to forget my own heart / While I tell you 'love is strange'….

Dreaming

Now the pigs are flying
And the people's voice is heard
Politicians do what's right
And work and wealth are shared
You can make it happen
You can make it true
It's easy when you're dreaming
There's nothing you can't do…

Now the war is over
And the children all get toys
Lots of choices for the girls
And no guns for the boys
You can make it happen
You can make it true
It's easy when you're dreaming
There's nothing you can't do…

You can make it happen
You can make it true
Dreaming / Dreaming / Dreaming…

Now the rich are sharing
And the starving all get fed
Fair-trade terms for Africa
And sugar on their bread
You can make it happen
You can make it true
It's easy when you're dreaming
There's nothing you can't do…

Evil ways are set in stone
That's how it sometimes seems
But if there's any hope of change
It starts from people's dreams…

You can make it happen
You can make it true
Dreaming / Dreaming / Dreaming….

Motel Interlude

We drove into the desert / And found a place to hide
A motel called the cactus tree / As dark as thought inside
Ev'rywhere I cared to look / Reminded me of us
Motel with its paint peeled off / And sidings gone to rust…

We sat in the cantina / Ate chilli dog with fries
Something seemed to catch her throat / And tears came to her eyes
Ev'rything I used to feel / Was welling in my heart
Motel holding both of us / A million miles apart…

People think a change of place
Will somehow change their fate
They think they'd better hit the road
Before it gets too late…

Got back to this crummy room / And lay down on the bed
To say the things that matter / But only in our heads
Ev'ry word that might have helped / So heavy with regret
Motel room where sleep won't come / We lie awake and sweat…

People think a change of place
Will somehow change their fate
They think they'd better hit the road
Before it gets too late…

People think a change of place
Will somehow change their luck
It's why so many hit the road
When life begins to suck…

We went out in the morning / And handed back the key
Neither of us has a clue / 'bout how things ought to be
Nothing certain up ahead / But more weight for the load
One check in the rear-view and / We're headed down the road….

Fever Tree

Shaking like a fever tree
Burning like the branch
I held you through your longest night
Yet I was in your debt
You found a use for someone lost
And for his aching limbs
You made me fight and breathe for you
And bathed me in your sweat…

Breaking like a sudden storm
Driving like the rain
You talked me through a pack of lies
But I was on your side
You'd given me another voice
And diff'rent things to feel
You made me glad the wheels still turned
And took me for a ride…

Strange how you fell in with me / The shaking of the fever tree…

And if you're bound to steal away / Make sure you steal it all…

You know the doors I leave unlocked / Make sure you steal it all…

Visiting these autumn days
Sometimes, like the sun
You bring me things that can't be kept
But I will take the hurt
You'll give me when the time is right
To show your work's complete
We found the guts all beauty needs
To rise out of the dirt…

Shaking like the fever tree
Burning like the branch
Won't let their grubby fingers touch
The bond that sets us free
We've been as real as any truth
That holy fools can learn
You'll make it to the farthest shore
And leave this heart to yearn….

For The Stars

You don't remember when you lost your way
You hid it from yourself until today
But now you feel the road is calling you
There's something that you always meant to do…

You're restless and you know the feeling's wrong
Still searching and you know you must move on
Some broken fences you can't hope to mend
The road can sometimes seem your only friend…

The road is more than girls and guitars
The road knows all your sorrows and scars
But the road goes on heading for the stars
For the stars
For the stars…

You're gambling but you know you lack the skill
Like time itself you know you can't be still
Some people see right through your poker face
You're losing 'cause you know you're out of place…

You're faking and it's time that you got real
Stop hiding from the deepest things you feel
It's time to leave your comfort zone behind
And live the dream that's always in your mind….

Points For Style

You get a six-point-six from the Russian judge
But a six-point-five from me
'cause you lose it when you give it all
And there's no-one else can see
That you wear a frozen smile
As they give you points for style…

You wear the skimpy clothes and the kinky boots
And they answer to the whip
You play the parts they demand of you
And you never let it slip
That the things they do are vile
As they give you points for style…

You hide a hunted look and you try to smile
But it doesn't reach your eyes
Despise yourself for what you've become
Since they sold you on their lies
When you're poor, life is a trial
But they give you points for style…

They don't know the value / And they don't care what it costs…
They don't know the hollow place / That echoes with your loss…

There's someone new and younger / To replace you in a while
Who gives a damn for substance when / What counts is points for style
Who gives a damn for flesh and blood / What counts is points for style…

You hide those unshed tears and you feign a laugh
To make others feel OK
To feed the child you were parted from
You'll do anything they say
Without choice, life is a trial
But they give you points for style…

When you're poor, life is a trial
But they give you points for style….

Way Back In The Trees

Way back in the trees
Way back in the trees
It doesn't live
But it breathes…

Way back in the trees
Way back in the trees
It doesn't grow
But it feeds..

And hides the things that we've done
And hides our sins from the sun…

Way back in the trees
Way back in the trees
It doesn't care
But it keeps
It doesn't sow
But it reaps…

And takes the lost to its heart
And takes the sting from the dart…

And holds the worst of our times
And seeps the stain of our crimes…

Way back in the trees
Way back in the trees
It doesn't live
But it breathes
It doesn't look
But it sees…

And hides the clues in the deep
And lulls the hours into sleep…

Way back in the trees
Way back in the trees
It doesn't thirst
But it drinks…

Though you hoped to forget
Peace hasn't come for you yet
Though you hoped to move on
There's always a witness
Who knows what you've done…

Way back in the trees
Way back in the trees
It doesn't move
But it waits…

And turns the knife into rust
And turns the years into dust…

And hides the blood in the leaves
And hides our guilt in the trees…

And turns the day into night
And turns the grief into sight
And turns the pain into light…

Way back in the trees
Way back in the trees
It doesn't sleep
But it wakes
It doesn't need
But it takes
It doesn't need
But it takes…

Way back in the trees….

Zeitgeist

When your time's become a ghost
And your icons are a host
Of legends
Who have gathered in the sky…

When the mirror shows a face
That has clearly run its race
With features
You no longer recognise…

Zeitgeist
Own up to the meaning
Zeitgeist
Face up to the feeling
If you're lucky / There's still love
There's nothing left for you / But love…

There are no roads left to run
That will take you to the sun
Or help you
To atone for crimes denied…

There are two ways you can turn
You can rise or you can burn
With longing
You can never satisfy…

Zeitgeist
Own up to the meaning
Zeitgeist
Face up to the feeling
If you're lucky / There's still love
There's nothing left for you / But love…

When it's hard to take the fight
To the enemies of light
Remember
It's still good to be alive…

It's still good to be alive….

Hobo Signs

Make me a mark on a boxcar wall
Leave me a message only we can read
Let me know where the welcome's good
For the last-born son of a dying breed…

Gone with the wind to the old east coast
Gone from Atlanta all ways up to Maine
Spent some time with a brown-eyed girl
knowing soon I'd be turning south again…

A hobo heart and hobo signs
Will always bring me back to you
And that other world across the tracks
For a tokay blanket and a mulligan stew
A tokay blanket and a burger too…

Seen ev'ry state where the railroad runs
Met all kinds of people across the land
There's more to life than work and pay
More signs than they will ever understand…

Meet me up at Britt before the fall
Let me fill your glass and we'll praise the grain
Still time to take some other trails
Till we have to catch that westbound train…

Still time to take some happy trails
Till we have to catch that westbound train…

Make me a mark on a boxcar wall
Leave me a message only we can read
Let me know where the welcome's good
For the last-born son a of a dying breed….

Twilight

I found you without looking
I turned and met your stare
Who knows how much the world had changed
Since you'd been standing there…

I meet you as a silence
Within this endless noise
You walk a rope above the crowd
No safety net but poise…

You spoke once of a fusion
You thought you'd never find
Believing no-one else down here
Is of the twilight kind…

You know your dream has called me
Beguiles this space and time
Come share with me the final peak
That love is made to climb…

We spoke once in a market
A thousand nights ago
And to your mind mine was the twin
You'd always sought to know…

Come ride away from madmen
Who've vowed to spill our blood
From pig-faced politicians now
Stood rooting in the mud…

Come ride from lands where gamblers
Throw pearls before such swine
Come ride in rags, a refugee
Who's bound to cross the line…

You want to place a feeling
You're not supposed to know
But find inside you have the strength
To let that passion grow…

Come ride at last through swamplands
Where alligators lust
And veil your face for deserts wide
Where history is dust…

Come ride away from failures
Who've vowed to give us hurt
Come ride and hold your head above
The cowards and their dirt…

We'll spark a realm of making
We'll join a velvet tribe
And green the way that leads to where
A diff'rent life can thrive…

Reject their world of violence
As phoney as it's bland
Against the lies of daylight thieves
We'll always make a stand…

Come ride with me through forests
Of disembodied eyes
Come ride with me through darkness deep
And take me as your prize…

We spoke once in your doorway
A hundred lives ago
And to my fate yours was the twin
But then we couldn't know…

Come ride with me where hunters
Have vowed to run us through
Come side with love that laughs at doom
And keeps on holding true…

Come ride in silk, a princess
Or bearing Aaron's rod
And satin-robed, a high priestess
Who doesn't heed a god…

Be with me fearing no-one
Feast with a wilder clan
Come find the ways to higher ground
And I will be your man…

We'll make a life creating
A beauty that will grow
You'll maybe touch great mysteries
So deep within the flow…

Be with me in a future
Where each can make their mark
Survivors and immortal ones
From lives without a spark…

Come ride with me from duties
Far better left undone
Come sail the ocean of the night
Eclipse the rising sun…

Don't flame out in the dawn light
Your dreams let fall like trash
The new moon brings another world
So far from wind-blown ash…

Come bide with me where freed souls
Give with an open hand
Look back at cities burning down
Once deemed the promised land…

Come bide with me where freed souls
Know what is built on sand
Look back at cities burning down
Once deemed the promised land….

From A Basement On A Hill   (for Elliott Smith)

The openness of music
The opacity of words
Obtuseness of the human heart
The simpleness of birds
Amazed that you could touch them
What you could make them feel
The spider in a web of tape
From a basement on a hill…

The mystery of being
Elasticity of time
The blink-and-miss-him poet's life
Eternity of rhyme
Surprised that you could sing it
And singing made it real
The laughter of a crazy man
From a basement on a hill…

Sometimes the light fades quickly
It leaves us in the dark
But if it turns out life / Is just a day
At least you made your mark
Sometimes the road to heaven
Can pass too close to hell
But if it turns out life / Is just a game
At least you played it well…

A rising to creation
And not flinching when it scars
To blaze like something dying, but
Sustaining like the stars
Amazed your role was central
The wheel within a wheel
The prism in a ray of light
From a basement on a hill…

Surprised that you could reach out
What you could make us feel
The mirror of a moment's grace
From a basement on a hill….

45

Scent Of Pine

When I've had a good day
And I'm walking on the water
Feeding the five thousand
Turning water into wine
I know you'll remind me
That I'm living in a cabin
A no-one going nowhere
Within the scent of pine…

When I've conquered Berlin
Taken Warsaw, entered Moscow
Changed the face of Europe
Because I received the sign
I know you'll remind me
That I never left Nevada
My hand inside my jacket
Within the scent of pine…

Snow on the sierras / Gleaming in the sunlight
Footprints of coyotes / Coming down the trails
Need you here beside me / To share a scent of freedom
I ask so much of your love / Hope it never fails…

When I was in the woods
And I thought I'd met the green men
Helped them find their saucer
When in fact I'd lost my mind
I'm glad you could reach me
Talk me down from off the ceiling
Only you can keep me safe
Within the scent of pine…

Once I lived in Vegas
And my mind was always speeding
Barely eating, sleeping
Yet still thinking I was fine
You showed me the city
Can look better from a distance
Seen from a night-dark mountain
Within the scent of pine….

Me And Brother Holden

You get so tired of falling
Through the nightmare of the phoney
Finding nothing down there
To convince you that your real
And no sign there to show
You'll ever get the chance to grow
And why they're so afraid of what we feel…

You get so choked at working
In a system that's a prison
Wanting nothing from them
Or their sick society
Except a reason why
So many people have to cry
And why they're so afraid we might get free…

I'll struggle with the madness / Hope you're somewhere doing great
You'll handle things your own way / I'm always just too late
Too late to find that state of grace / While barely getting by
So it's me and brother Holden / Simply catchers in the rye…

Me and brother Holden / Simply catchers in the rye…

You get so burned from striving
In the homeland of seductions
Boxes of all sizes
holding emptiness that's all
But hoping someone there
knows what the greedy never share
And why they're so afraid they're gonna fall…

You get so fazed by searching
For a way to cross the border
Seeing nothing changing
That would make you want to stay
And why the gentlest yet
Are seen as such a mortal threat…

And why they're so afraid we'll get away….

Two Kids

Joseph came to Vegas from the west coast
Sophie simply wanted to be free
They only had to meet
For their world to seem complete
Together was the perfect place to be…

Joseph went to work at a casino
Sophie cleaned up rooms at the motel
They had themselves a team
They set out to live their dream
And for a while they made out pretty well…

Sophie wouldn't talk about her past life
How she came to run away from home
But Joseph held her close
The future's what counts the most
The past was somewhere shivered through alone…

Joseph had the confidence of ten men
All his plans were built on solid ground
Made Sophie feel secure
Knowing she was loved for sure
She felt her life was fin'lly turning round…

Sophie's parents said she'd been abducted
Had detectives lookin' for the proof
They put Joe in the cage
Said that she was under-age
But Sophie made them listen to the truth…

Joseph took his turn down at the court house
Sophie's words made sure they set him free
They'll always be a team
And won't give up on their dream
The world will one day have to let them be…

Joseph lost his job at the casino
Though the boss agreed he'd done no wrong
'Our good name in the press
Is the key to our success'
Hypocrisy and Justice don't get on…

Joe's back with his people up in 'Frisco
Sophie rings the same time ev'ry day
They're counting down the time
When loving will be no crime
And they'll be one and simply fly away….

Yellow Moon

Yellow moon
Alone in the darkness
Reflecting light
On the madness of man
Is looking down
At human pollution
A jaundiced eye
On the lack of a plan…

Yellow moon
Alone in the distance
Throws a cold light
On the sickness of greed
And has a view
On encroachment by deserts
Is never blind
To the causes of need…

Yellow moon / yellow moon
What you've seen / yellow moon…

Yellow moon
Alone in the silence
Turns mirror light
On the guard and the fence
The smallest part
Of vast waste by the wealthy
Tragic motif
Of their absence of sense…

Yellow moon
Alone in the darkness
Reflected light
On the dinosaurs' birth
And later looked
At the dull and unheeding
A falling rock
Simply wiped from the earth.…

Wherever Frankie Runs

Wherever Frankie runs
All kinds of mayhem tends to follow
'cause she's searching for the truth
And she just won't be denied
So I'm with her all the way
'cause I know the price that you pay
When at last you're facing down the ones who lied…

Wherever Frankie stands
She takes the high ground of the hero
And if someone has to fall
It means they've been doing wrong
So she seems like kin to me
'cause I know how hard it can be
When you have to lose so much but stay so strong…

Whenever Frankie hurts
You know unnumbered hearts ache with her
'cause all who look for justice
Surely recognise her pain
Though she's got so far to go
Yet I hope somehow that she'll know
That I'm standing there beside her in the rain…

So wherever she leads
And whatever she needs
Though she might ask for the heat
Of a thousand suns
Whatever she may want
At whatever the cost
I want to be
Wherever Frankie runs…

Wherever Frankie goes
A lot of loving will go with her
'cause she's lifted up a torch
And so many need the light
So it would be like a dream
To be caught up in her slipstream
And to be around when wrong is turned to right….

Land Of Dreams

When I got out of nowhere
The road I took went west
Through mining towns and steel towns
All seeming past their best
Run-down diners, empty motels
That could use a lick of paint
Where some might see a kind of romance
Although their really ain't…

When I came to the mountains
The road began to climb
Through awesome buttes and boulders
That seemed as old as time
But no-one there had work for me
And I knew I couldn't stay
Still the road stretched out a thousand miles
So I went on my way…

This used to be a land of dreams / And dreamers led the way
But look around and tell me, friend / Who holds the keys today?
Big money runs the country / Some people live in fear
Too many lives have been foreclosed / And the future isn't clear…

Came to a metropolis
That sprawled beside the sea
I joined a crowd of hopefuls
Got called a 'wannabe'
Now it's only by permission
That we get a chance to shine
So I'm sitting, dreaming in the sun
And waiting to get mine…

I've come to the conclusion
This empire has to fall
Got to find a better way
A fairer life for all
People living with frustration
Never get the chance to grow
All those dreams backed up along the shore
With nowhere left to go….

Coming Up From Nothing

Cotton in the country
But satin in the penthouse
Or pin-striped for the city
If that's what it should take
I'll follow in your footsteps
While you realise your power
Want to be beside you
In the moment that you wake…

Coming up from nothing
And never going back there
You plan to keep on shining
Till they call you a star
I'll lift you if you stumble
'cause you've lost yourself in their lies
I'll be there beside you
To remind you who you are…

Coming up from nothing / So tired of being hungry
Coming up from nothing / And wond'ring what life's for
Coming up from nothing / That old familiar story
That old familiar story / So tired of being poor…

Freezing for the cam'ra
But fluid on the catwalk
And shifting shape comes easy
If that's the price of fame
I'll listen for the come down
In the cadence of your laughter
Try to be beside you
When you find it's all a game…

Coming up from nothing
And never going back there
You plan to go on fighting
You're bound to make the grade
I'll hold you when you're hurting
'cause you've found their world is phoney
I'll be there beside you
If the glitter starts to fade….

Hugo's Song

To a heart closed like a fist
You lift the open arms of childhood
Defy the logic of a dying world
Give it back a sense of fun
Another wide-eyed dream begun…

On those billboards standing tall
You'd share a loving smile with millions
Dispel the bitterness of ancient feuds
Give worn minds a hopeful sign
Remind the sun why it should shine…

Time to listen
To innocent voices
To laugh with children
And remember how to play
Reject adult rubbish
We're told is important
Protect their tomorrow
By changing today…

We might fake that Stepford look
And not contest what the liars say
Refuse to stand beside the helpless ones
But that's something we can't do
Each to their own self will be true…

To those hearts closed like a fist
You open trusting as a flower
Inspire commitment without needing words
Make us face up to what's wrong
Can't shut our ears to Hugo's song…

Make us stand up to what's wrong
Can't close our minds to Hugo's song….

Fall From Grace

There's nothing in the moonlight
Shining on the road
To show / Which way she might have gone
There's nothing in the stillness
Silencing the trees
To tell / The one who follows
What's been done
There's nothing in an empty heart
To measure out the cost
Or feel another's growing sense of loss…

There's nowhere you can turn to
Searching in the book
To find / A single reason why
There's nowhere in the dawn light
Hurting sleepless eyes
To show / A hopeful pathway
You could try
There's nowhere in a fall from grace
To stand out of the rain
While knowing it's yourself you have to blame…

There's nothing but the pathways
Through the forest
Nothing but the moonlight
On the road…

There's nothing in the moonlight
Shining on the road
To show / Which way she might have gone
There's nothing in the sullen
Absence of a breeze
To tell / The one who's falling
What went wrong
There's nothing in a guilty heart
To measure out the cost
Or feel another lover's sense of loss….

Wild With Me

In my wildest dreams
Creating is the key
I'd give it all for such a life
What I call being free
Hoping you lean that way too
With a need to make
That must come through
To the glories that could be
If you'd be wild with me…

If this world of stone
Begins to weigh you down
At least you have a way to go
No need to wear a frown
Throw off moods so drab and dark
Touch an open hand
And feel the spark
Of the glories that could be
If you'd be wild with me…

When my mind breaks free
And sorrows can't intrude
I get to be my old best self
Enhancing brighter moods
Painting with an ease and touch
For the boldest minds
That long so much
For the glories that could be
If you'd be wild with me…

Won't there come a time
You'll want to turn and run
From all the empty lives and lies
From all the wrong that's done
To a place beyond the reach
Of the coldest skills
That world can teach
To the glories that could be
If you'd be wild with me…

When you come at last
There's nothing I won't do
To help you make glass ceilings smash
Get where you're going to
Such a hope is only shared
By the bravest hearts
That live to dare
And could really come to be
If you'd be wild with me….

To All The Dreamers

Sitting at the back of a greyhound bus
Sitting at the back of a greyhound bus
Your instinct says keep moving
'cause the boom has turned to bust...

Thinking 'bout a girl and some things you'd planned
Thinking 'bout a girl and some things you'd planned
You know you're gonna miss her
But you hope she'll understand...

Praying you were right when you headed west
Praying you were right when you headed west
You're California dreaming
And you're hoping for the best...

California dreaming
In the USA
Raise a glass to all the dreamers
That'll hit the road today...

Sitting at the back of a greyhound bus
Sitting at the back of a greyhound bus
The future may look hopeful
But the past is so much dust...

The future may look hopeful
But the past is so much dust....

Mama Wolf

When I was still a mama wolf
My nature was to nurture
To guard you with my life itself
Let nothing near to hurt you…

I'd tumble you with gentle paws
And let you learn from playing
Until a restless time had come
And each was set on straying…

Then slowly I was turned from love
And saw the world was changing
With jagged glass and concrete shards
A scene that felt estranging…

I wandered in a summer world
Expecting life and leisure
But found a place of drudgery
And regimented pleasures…

I wandered in a wintry world
That froze the heart inside me
And marvelled at humanity
Its leaders and their cruelty…

So many skies have turned since then
And many new suns risen
I want to see my cubs again
And feel my heart beat with them…

'cause you still know my darling babes
While moonlight shines upon you
You only have to raise the call
There's nothing that I won't do…

'cause you still know my darling ones
That you will find my heart true
To lift you in your hardest times
And I will always love you….

About the Writer

Martin J. White was born in Winchester, Hampshire but moved many times during a childhood that was frequently so traumatic that his writing can be considered survivor's poetry. He finally gained the opportunity to share real affection and personal growth by escaping to Yorkshire and London, spending time on the fringes of the music scene.

Settling in Swansea in October 1992, he became active as a supporter of the charity Butterfly Conservation, of which he has now been a Branch Committee member for more than 25 years. As such, he has discovered several moth species new to Wales and contributed to the efforts to map & conserve some of the best habitats and rarest insect species in Britain.

Martin has also spent decades as an active campaigner in defense of the NHS, against the Poll Tax, for free education and on many other issues and in more recent years, has worked as a volunteer in the Oxfam book shop in Castle Street, Swansea.

Martin harboured the ambition to be a songwriter from an early age (this dream coming second only to the desire to be a painter) and the lyrics included here are a selection from a very much larger body of work that includes a large body of poetry and an as-yet-unpublished book of animal stories. The newer lyrics in this collection were intended to function both as songs (with instrumental accompaniment) or as performance poetry to be read aloud; but each of these lyrics has a working melody.

For several years Martin was very active in the excellent critical writer's workshops in Huddersfield, which Ian McMillan called 'the poetry capital' of the north of England. In addition to his earlier collection 'My Heart Blown Open Wide' (Hafan Books, 2005), he has had poems published in a number of anthologies and such magazines as *Orbis, Weyfarers, The Echo Room, Roundyhouse, Iota* and *Poetry Wales*.

Martin would be pleased to receive any feedback about these lyrics (especially genuine & potentially lucrative offers of collaboration!) at:

martinjohnwhite@googlemail.com